Lots of Animal jokes for kids

Also by Whee Winn

Lots of Jokes for Kids
Lots of Knock-Knock Jokes for Kids
The Super, Epic, Mega Joke Book for Kids
Lots of Christmas Jokes for Kids
Lots of Tongue Twisters for Kids
Lots of Jokes and Riddles Box Set
On the Go Jokes for Kids

Lots of Animal jokes for kids

ZONDER**kidz**™

ZONDERKIDZ

Lots of Animal Jokes for Kids
Copyright © 2020 by Zondervan

Requests for information should be addressed to:
Zonderkidz, 3900 *Sparks Dr. SE, Grand Rapids, Michigan* 49546

Library of Congress Cataloging-in-Publication Data

Names: Winn, Whee, author.
Title: Lots of animal jokes for kids / by Whee Winn.
Description: Grand Rapids: Zonderkidz, 2020. | Audience: Ages 6–10
Summary: "Lots of Animal Jokes for Kids includes hilarious jokes for
    kids for endless hours of entertainment at a can't-be-beat price"—
    Provided by publisher.
Identifiers: LCCN 2019038466 | ISBN 9780310769521 (paperback) |
    ISBN 9780310769538 (epub)
Subjects: LCSH: Animals—Juvenile humor. | Wit and humor, Juvenile.
Classification: LCC PN6231.A5 W56 2020 | DDC 818/.602—dc23
LC record available at https://lccn.loc.gov/2019038466

Interior design: Denise Froehlich

Printed in the United States of America

20 21 22 23 24 /LSC/ 10 9 8 7 6 5 4 3 2 1

Note to Kids

Looking for some fun? Want to be silly? Giggle a little? Belly laugh? Then you've come to the right place. We have done all the work for you—we put together the perfect collection of jokes, riddles, tongue twisters, knock-knock jokes, and one-liners about farm animals, pets, snakes, birds, safari creatures, ocean and water animals, all things zoo, and a special bonus section on dinosaurs. And this collection is even more special because every joke in here is good for everyone . . . from your best friends to your parents to your teachers. *Lots of Animal Jokes for Kids* is just the place to find good old clean and corny jokes to entertain your friends for hours.

Contents

1

Pet Puns

How do you know when it's raining cats and dogs?
You step in a poodle.

How can you tell which rabbits are getting old?
Look for the grey hares.

Why are cats good at video games?
Because they have nine lives!

How do you stop a dog barking in the back seat of a car?
Put him in the front seat.

What's a cat's favorite color?
Purr-ple.

What goes tick-tock, bow-wow, tick-tock, bow-wow?
A watchdog.

Where do rabbits go after their wedding?
On their bunny-moon.

Knock, knock.
Who's there?
Tyler.
Tyler who?
Tyler dog up or he'll run away.

How does a dog stop a video?
He presses the paws button.

My dog has no nose!
How does he smell?
Terrible.

When is it bad luck to see a black cat?
When you're a mouse.

What do you do if your dog chews a dictionary?
Take the words right out of his mouth.

Why don't cats like online shopping?
They prefer to use a cat-alogue.

What is the difference between fleas and dogs?
Dogs can have fleas, but fleas can't have dogs.

What do you call a cold dog sitting on top of a bunny?
A chili dog on a bun.

What time is it when five dogs chase one cat?
Five after one.

What kind of dog can do magic tricks?
A labracadabrador.

What game did the cat like to play with the mouse?
Catch!

How is a dog like a telephone?
It has a collar I.D.

Knock, knock.
Who's there?
Patsy.
Patsy who?
Patsy dog on the head—he likes it!

**What did the dog say when
it sat on sandpaper?**
"Ruff!"

**There were ten cats in a boat and one
jumped out. How many were left?**
None—they were all copycats.

What is a dog's favorite instrument?
A trombone.

**How do you know that carrots
are good for your eyesight?**
Because you never see a rabbit wearing glasses.

Have you ever seen a catfish?
No, how did it hold the rod?

Where do you put barking dogs?
In a barking lot.

**What do you get when you cross
a dog and a calculator?**
A friend you can really count on.

What did the clean dog say to the insect?
"Long time, no flea."

**What happened to the dog that
ate nothing but garlic?**
His bark was much worse than his bite!

Knock, knock.
Who's there?
Yvette.
Yvette who?
**Yvette helps a lot
of sick pets.**

What do you get when you cross a cocker spaniel, a poodle, and a rooster?
A Cockerpoodledoo.

What is the unluckiest kind of cat to have?
A cat-astrophe.

Why do dogs run in circles?
Because it's hard to run in squares.

Why did the dog cross the road twice?
He was trying to fetch a boomerang.

When is the best time to buy budgies?
When they're going cheep.

What dog keeps the best time?
A watchdog.

**How does a mouse feel after
it takes a shower?**
Squeaky clean.

Why did the kitten go to medical school?
To become a first aid kit.

Why did the poor dog chase his tail?
He was trying to make both ends meet.

Knock, knock.
Who's there?
Howl.
Howl who?
Howl you know unless you open the door?

What do cats like to eat on a hot day?
Mice cream.

What is the quietest kind of dog?
A hush puppy.

What kind of dog always runs a fever?
A hot dog!

What's a dog's favorite breakfast food?
Pooched eggs.

What do you do if your cat swallows your pencil?
Use a pen.

How do you say goodbye to a curly-haired dog?
Poodle-oo!

What happens when a cat eats a lemon?
It becomes a sour puss!

Where did the cat go when it lost its tail?
To the retail store!

**What is the difference between a
dog and a marine biologist?**
One wags a tail and the other tags a whale.

Where did the kittens go on their field trip?
The mewseum.

**What's a rabbit's
favorite dance style?**
Hip-hop.

How do you get a dog to stop digging in the garden?
Take away his shovel.

Why don't dogs make good dancers?
Because they have two left feet.

What's a cat's way of keeping law and order?
Claw enforcement.

What did the waiter say when he brought out the dog's dinner?
"Bone appétit!"

Knock, knock.
Who's there?
Some bunny.
Some bunny who?
Some bunny has been eating all my carrots!

Why do dogs wag their tails?
Because no one else will do it for them.

What bug does a cat sleep on?
A caterpillow.

What's a mouse's favorite game?
Hide and squeak.

What type of markets do dogs avoid?
Flea markets!

What is a cat's favorite movie?
The Sound of Meow-sic!

What kind of dog loves to take bubble baths?
A shampoodle.

What happened when the cat ate a ball of yarn?
She had mittens.

What's a puppy's favorite kind of pizza?
Pupperoni.

Why was the cat afraid of a tree?
Because of the bark!

What kind of dog is all bark and no bite?
A dogwood.

What is a cat's favorite song?
Three Blind Mice.

Why are cats so loveable?
Because they are purr-fect.

What do you call a dog that is left handed?
A south paw!

What did the cowboy say when his dog ran away?
Well, doggone!

What does a cat say when somebody steps on its tail?
Me-ow!

2

Farmyard Funnies

Why does a rooster watch TV?
For hen-tertainment!

How do rabbits travel?
By hareplane.

What do you get from a pampered cow?
Spoiled milk.

Where do rabbits eat breakfast?
IHOP.

Why was the chicken sick?
It had the people pox.

What do you get from a nervous cow?
A milkshake.

**What do you call farm animals
that have a sense of humor?**
Laughing stock.

What does a mixed-up hen lay?
Scrambled eggs.

Why did the pony have to gargle?
Because he was a little horse.

**What do you call a
crate full of ducks?**
A box of quackers.

Knock, knock.
Who's there?
Barbara.
Barbara who?
Barbara, black sheep, have you any wool?

What do you call a pig that's been arrested for dangerous driving?
A road hog.

Why did the chicken cross the road, roll in the mud, and cross the road again?
Because it was a dirty double-crosser.

**What do you call a group of
rabbits hopping backwards?**
A receding hare line.

What animal grows down as it grows up?
A duck.

What do you call a cow that eats your grass?
A lawn moo-er.

Why did the lamb cross the road?
To get to the baaaaarber shop!

What has four legs and goes "Oom, Oom?"
A cow walking backwards!

**What happened when 500 hares
got loose on Main Street?**
The police had to comb the area.

Why did the sheep get pulled over on the freeway?
Because she did a ewe-turn.

What's the most musical part of a chicken?
The drumstick.

What do you call a pig that does karate?
A pork chop.

A sheep, a drum, and a snake fall off a cliff. What sound do they make?
Baa-dum-tsssss.

A duck, a skunk, and a deer went out for dinner at a restaurant one night.
When it came time to pay, the skunk didn't have a scent and the deer didn't have a buck, so they put the meal on the duck's bill.

What did the horse say when he fell?
"I've fallen, and I can't giddy up!"

**What is the easiest way to
count a herd of cattle?**
Use a cowculator.

**What do you get when you cross
an opossum and a bull?**
Don't be silly—that's opossum-bull.

**What do you get
when you cover a
pig with needles?**
A pork-upine.

Why do cows go to New York City?
To see the moosicals.

What do you call a bunch of chickens playing hide-and-seek?
Fowl play.

What do you call an arctic cow?
An In-moo-it.

What is a bunny's motto?
Don't be mad, be hoppy!

What do you give a pig with a rash?
Oinkment.

What animal says "quick, quick?"
A duck with hiccups.

Knock, knock.
Who's there?
Alpaca.
Alpaca who?
Alpaca the suitcase, you load up the car.

There are two cows in a paddock.
One of them says, "Moo!"
The other one says, "Hey, that's what I was going to say."

What do you call a chicken at the North Pole?
Lost.

What do you call a twitchy cow?
Beef jerky.

What do you get when you cross fireworks and a duck?
Firequackers.

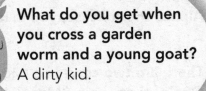

What do you get when you cross a garden worm and a young goat?
A dirty kid.

What do you call a rabbit who is angry over getting sunburnt?
A hot cross bunny.

Why did the cow cross the road?
To get to the udder side.

Why did the chicken cross the clothing store?
To get to the other size.

What is a horse's favorite sport?
Stable tennis!

What would happen if pigs could fly?
The price of bacon would go up.

Where do sheep go to get their wool cut?
The baa-baa shop.

I was going to tell you a cow joke . . .
. . . but it's pasture bedtime.

What do you call it when it rains chickens and ducks?
Fowl weather.

When does a horse talk?
Whinny wants to.

What do you call a cow in a tornado?
A milkshake!

Where do horses go when they get sick?
To the horsepital.

What do ducks like to eat with soup?
Quackers.

Why did the man stand behind the horse?
He was hoping to get a kick out of it.

**Why did the chicken cross
the basketball court?**
It heard the referee was calling fowls.

**What's black and white, black and
white, black and white and green?**
Three skunks fighting over a pickle!

What do you call a pig with no legs?
A groundhog.

Knock, knock.
Who's there?
Goat.
Goat who?
Goat to the door and find out!

What do you get when you cross a sheepdog with a rose?
Collie-flower.

Why do cows wear bells around their necks?
Because their horns don't work.

What does it mean if you find a horseshoe?
Some poor horse is walking around in his socks.

Where did the duck go when he was sick?
To see the ducktor.

What do you call a dancing sheep?
A baallerina.

Why shouldn't you tell secrets to a cow?
Because it goes in one ear and out the udder.

**What do you call a horse
that lives next door?**
A neigh-bor!

Why are rabbits so lucky?
They have four rabbit's feet?

Which side of a duck has the most feathers?
The outside.

**A man rode his horse into town on
Friday. The next day, he rode back
on Friday. How is this possible?**
His horse's name is Friday.

Knock, knock.
Who's there?
Cows go.
Cows go who?
No, silly, cows go "moo!"

Why do hens lay eggs?
If they dropped them, they'd break.

**What kind of mouse does not
eat, drink, or even walk?**
A computer mouse.

**What do you call a duck that steals
the soap from the bath?**
A robber ducky.

What was the first animal in space?
The cow that jumped over the moon.

What do you call a sheep covered in chocolate?
A candy baa.

What do you call a clever duck?
A wise-quacker.

There were two cows in a field.
The first cow said, "Moo!"
The second cow said, "Baa!"
The first cow asked the second cow, "Why did you say baa?"
The second cow said, "I'm learning a foreign language."

What do ducks like to watch on TV?
Duckumentaries.

What allergy do horses fear the most?
Hay fever.

What do you get when a chicken lays an egg on top of a barn?
An eggroll.

What do you call a pig with three eyes?
A piiig.

If chickens rise when the rooster crows, when do ducks wake up?
At the quack of dawn.

How many sheep does it take to knit a sweater?
Don't be silly—sheep can't knit!

3

Silly
Safari

Where does an elephant pack his luggage?
In his trunk.

**What time is it when an elephant
sits on the fence?**
Time to fix the fence!

Why do giraffes have long necks?
Because their feet smell.

What do you give an elephant with big feet?
Plenty of room.

**Why did the lion spit
out the clown?**
Because he tasted funny.

What do you get when you cross an elephant and a kangaroo?
Really big holes all over Australia.

What's a lion's favorite state?
Maine.

What happens to hippos when they get too cold?
They get hippothermia.

Why are giraffes so slow to apologize?
It takes them a long time to swallow their pride.

What's big and gray and keeps you dry in the rain?
An umbrelephant.

Why didn't the boy believe the tiger?
He thought it was a lion.

What's gray and turns red?
An embarrassed rhinoceros.

How do monkeys get down the stairs?
They slide down the bananaster.

What would you do if an elephant sat in front of you at a movie?
Miss most of the film.

What kind of music do hippos like?
Hippo-hop.

**Why shouldn't you play cards
on the African savannah?**
Because of all the cheetahs there.

What do you get when two giraffes collide?
A giraffic jam.

**What lizard do you get if you
cross a camel and a lion?**
A chameleon.

**How do you catch
a monkey?**
Climb a tree and act
like a banana.

What's as big as an elephant but weighs nothing?
Its shadow.

How does a lion greet other animals on a safari?
"Nice to eat you!"

What's the difference between a tiger and a lion?
The tiger has the mane part missing.

How can you get a hippo to do whatever you want?
Hippo-notism.

Knock, knock.
Who's there?
Rhino.
Rhino who?
Rhino every knock-knock joke there is!

What is big, gray, beautiful, and wears glass slippers?
Cinderelephant.

What do you call a tiny hippo that likes to eat cheese?
A hippopotamouse.

What is gray and blue and very big?
An elephant holding its breath!

What do cheetahs like to eat?
Fast food.

Why did the ant elope?
Nobody gnu.

What do you call a messy hippo?
A hippopota-mess!

What's invisible and smells like bananas?
Monkey toots.

What do you do with a blue elephant?
You try and cheer her up.

Would you rather have a tiger eat you or a lion?
I'd rather have the tiger eat the lion.

How do you stop a rhino from charging?
Take away his credit card.

What do you call a sloppy hippo?
A hippopota-mess.

When does a giraffe have eight legs?
When there are two of them.

What does a lion use to brush his mane?
A catacomb.

Why are elephants so wrinkled?
Have you ever tried to iron one?

What kind of key opens a banana?
A monkey.

**What did the lion say to her pride
before they went out hunting?**
"Let us prey."

**What did the peanut say
to the elephant?**
Nothing, peanuts don't talk.

**What kind of monkey flies
through the air?**
A hot air baboon.

What is the biggest ant in the world?
An eleph-ant.

**What has two tails, three
horns, and six feet?**
A rhino with spare parts.

What's green and
hangs from trees?
Giraffe snot.

**What did the
banana do when the
monkey chased it?**
The banana split.

**What are the oldest
animals in the world?**
Zebras—they're still in
black and white.

**What do you get when
you cross a squirrel
with an elephant?**
An animal that remembers
where it buries its nuts.

Why can't a leopard hide?
Because he's always spotted.

What do hippos make when they form a band?
Hippopotamusic.

What do you call an elephant in a phone booth?
Stuck.

What do you call an exploding monkey?
A baBOOM.

Knock, knock.
Who's there?
Giraffe.
Giraffe who?
Giraffe anything to eat? I'm starving!

Why did the monkey like the banana?
Because it had appeal.

**What happened when the
lion ate the comedian?**
He felt funny.

What do you call an angry elephant?
An earthquake.

What do you call a royal giraffe?
Your highness.

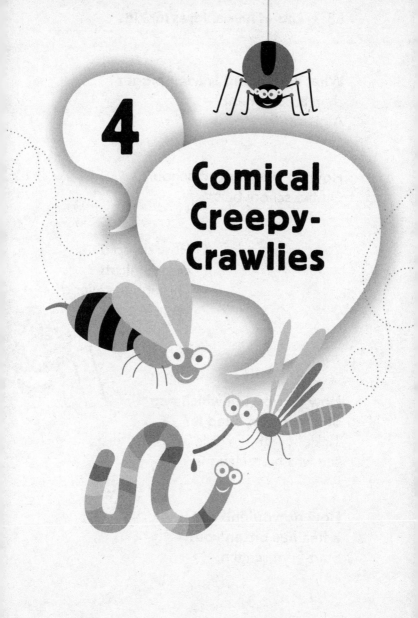

4

Comical Creepy-Crawlies

What kind of ant is even bigger than an elephant?
A gi-ant.

How do bees get to school?
On the school buzz.

How do spiders communicate?
Through the World Wide Web.

How do you tell which end of a worm its head is?
Tickle it in the middle and see which end laughs.

How do you find out if a flea has bitten you?
Start from scratch.

What's better than a talking dog?
A spelling bee.

Why did the bee go to the doctor?
Because he had hives.

What do you call a fly without wings?
A crawl.

Why do bees have sticky hair?
Because they use honeycombs.

What makes a glowworm glow?
A light meal.

What do you call a guard with 100 legs?
A sentrypede.

What has four wheels and flies?
A garbage truck.

How do fleas travel?
They itchhike.

Why are As like flowers?
Because bees come after them.

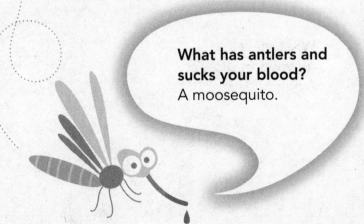

What has antlers and sucks your blood?
A moosequito.

**What kind of ant can
you color with?**
A crayant.

**What did the queen bee say
to the naughty bee?**
"Beehive yourself."

**What do you get when you cross
a parrot and a centipede?**
A walkie-talkie.

Knock, knock.
Who's there?
Honey bee.
Honey bee who?
Honey, be a dear and open the door!

What do you call a 100-year-old ant?
An ant-ique.

What kind of bee hums and drops things?
A fumble bee.

What did the bee say to the flower?
"Hello, honey!"

**What do you get when you cross
some ants with some ticks?**
All kinds of antics.

Why did the fly fly?
Because the spider
spied 'er.

What is black and yellow and buzzes along at 30,000 feet?
A bee in an airplane.

What has fifty legs but can't walk?
Half a centipede.

What does a queen bee do when she burps?
She issues a royal pardon.

Why is it good to keep a glowworm in your backpack?
It will lighten your load.

Knock, knock.
Who's there?
Abbie.
Abbie who?
Abbie just stung me! Ouch!

What do you call a snail on a ship?
A snailor.

Where do bees go on vacation?
Stingapore.

What did one flea say to the other at the end of the day?
"Should we walk or take a dog?"

What goes zzub, zzub?
A bee flying backwards.

Where would you put an injured insect?
In an antbulance.

What kind of bee can't be understood?
A mumble bee.

What is a bee's favorite flower?
Bee-gonias.

A team of little animals and a team of big animals decided to play football.

During the first half of the game, the big animals were winning. But during the second half, a centipede scored so many touchdowns that the little animals won the game.

When the game was over, the chipmunk asked the centipede, "Where were you during the first half?"

He replied, "Putting on my shoes!"

Where do ants go on vacation?
Frants.

Where do bees wait to get on public transportation?
At the buzz stop.

What do bees chew?
Bumblegum.

What insect runs away from everything?
A flee.

Who is a bee's favorite painter?
Pablo Beecasso.

What do you call an ant who likes to be alone?
Independ-ant.

What did one bee say to the other in the summer?
"Swarm in here, isn't it?"

How many bees do you need for a bee choir?
A humdred.

5

Absurd Birds

Why do hummingbirds hum?
Because they can't remember the words.

**What do you get when you
cross a parrot with a pig?**
A bird who hogs the conversation.

What do you call a cold penguin?
A brrrrd.

What's an owl's favorite type of math?
Owlgebra.

**What do you give
a sick bird?**
Tweetment.

A pelican and a toucan went out to dinner and ordered every item on the menu.
Their bills were huge!

Which bird is always out of breath?
A puffin.

How does a bird with a broken wing manage to land safely?
It uses its sparrowchute.

How does a penguin make pancakes?
With its flippers.

**Why was the duck put into
the basketball game?**
To make a fowl shot!

**Why does a flamingo lift
up one leg when it sleeps?**
Because if it lifted up both
legs, it would fall down.

Knock, knock.
Who's there?
Owl.
Owl who?
Owl see you later.

**What birds spend most of
their time in church?**
Birds of pray.

What bird can be heard at mealtime?
A swallow.

What do you call a woodpecker without a beak?
A headbanger.

Why do seagulls live by the sea?
Because if they lived by the bay, they would be bagels.

What is in a penguin's favorite salad?
Iceberg lettuce.

What do you call an owl with a deep voice?
A growl.

A police officer sees a man driving around with a pickup truck full of penguins.

He pulls the guy over and says, "You can't drive around with penguins in this town! Take them to the zoo immediately."

The guy agrees and drives away.

The next day, the officer sees the guy still driving around with the truck full of penguins. This time they're all wearing sunglasses.

He pulls the guy over and says, "I thought I told you to take these penguins to the zoo yesterday!"

The guy replies, "I did! Today I'm taking them to the beach."

Which bird is also a spoiled piece of fruit?
A pear-rot.

What is the opposite of a flamingo?
A flamingstop.

How do crows stick together in a flock?
Velcrow.

**How many birds does it take
to change a lightbulb?**
Toucan do it.

Why do penguins carry fish in their beaks?
Because they don't have pockets.

**Which seabird carries fish in its bill
and has a wick on its head?**
A pelicandle.

What kind of bird can open a door?
A turkey.

Why did the owl invite his friends over?
He didn't want to be owl by himself.

**What do you get when you cross
a parrot and a woodpecker?**
A bird that talks in Morse code.

What do you call a fabulous pink bird?
A glamingo.

**Did you hear the one about the
crow and the telephone pole?**
He wanted to make a long-distance caw.

What do you call an owl wearing armor?
A knight owl.

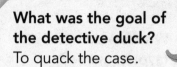

What was the goal of the detective duck?
To quack the case.

What do you call a heron that steals people's toupees?
A heroff.

What's the difference between a bird and a fly?
A bird can fly, but a fly can't bird.

What is black and white and red all over?
A sunburned penguin.

What do you call a courageous raven?
A braven.

What's a parrot's favorite game?
Hide-and-speak.

Knock, knock.
Who's there?
Who.
Who who?
What are you, an owl?

Which kind of bird never needs a comb?
A bald eagle.

How did the bird break into the house?
With a crow bar.

What time does a duck wake up?
At the quack of dawn!

Where do penguins go to see movies?
The dive-in.

How do flamingos meet new flamingos?
They flamingle.

What is black and white and black and white and black and white and . . . ?
A penguin falling down the stairs!

When does a teacher carry birdseed?
When there is a parrot-teacher conference!

What kind of bird works at a construction site?
The crane!

What do you call a funny chicken?
A comedi-hen

What bird is always sad?
The blue jay

What do ducks get after they eat?
A bill!

Why do birds fly south in the winter?
Because it's too far to walk!

How does a camel take a picture?
With a camelra.

What do you call a bear with no ear?
B.

**What sound do porcupines
make when they kiss?**
Ouch!

**What do you call a baby
bear with no teeth?**
A gummy bear!

Did you hear that a bunch of aquatic mammals got loose at the zoo?
It was otter chaos.

What happened when the wolf swallowed a clock?
He got ticks.

What is the first thing bats learn in school?
The alphabat.

Why are camels good at hiding?
They're great at camelflage.

What do Chinese bears eat for breakfast?
Pandacakes.

What do you call a little monkey who's just like his dad?
A chimp off the old block.

What did the buffalo say to his son when he left?
"Bison!"

What do you call a bear in the rain?
A drizzly bear.

What do you get when you cross a porcupine with a balloon?
POP!

Did you hear about the pandas that got into a food fight?
They all got bambooboos.

What's a good name for a straight-backed camel?
Humphrey.

Where does a tiger sleep?
Anywhere he wants!

What do you get when you cross a wolf and a sheep?
You have to get a new sheep.

How do you stop a skunk from smelling?
Plug its nose.

What kind of store does an ape own?
A monkey business.

What do you call a wolf that uses bad language?
A swearwolf.

What country do camels like to travel to?
Camelbodia.

What did the judge say when the skunk walked into the courtroom?
"Odor in the court!"

What do you get when you cross a hungry cat and a whole roast duck?
A duck-filled fatty-puss.

Knock, knock.
Who's there?
Chimp.
Chimp who?
I think it's pronounced "shampoo."

Why did the otter become an astronaut?
So he could go to otter space.

**What animal jumps when it walks
and sits when it stands?**
A kangaroo.

What is the fiercest flower in the garden?
A tiger lily.

**What do you call a monkey
who makes potato chips?**
A chipmunk.

Which animal is best at baseball?
A bat.

What do sloths make when it snows?
Slow angels.

**What's worse than a centipede
with athlete's foot?**
A porcupine with split ends.

Why do skunks celebrate Valentine's Day?
Because they are scent-imental.

How does one wolf greet another?
"Howl do you do?"

**How do you catch a fish
without a fishing pole?**
With your bear hands.

What's a kangaroo's favorite kind of candy?
Lollihops.

What do you call lending money to a bison?
A buffaloan.

Knock, knock.
Who's there?
Fangs.
Fangs who?
Fangs for letting me in!

An anteater walks into a restaurant.
The waiter asks, "Can I get you anything to drink?"
The anteater says, "Noooooooo."
"How about an appetizer?" the waiter asks.
The anteater says, "Noooooooo."
"Is there *anything* I can get you?" the waiter asks.
Again, the anteater says, "Noooooooo."
Frazzled, the waiter asks, "What's with the long noes?"
The anteater replies, "I was born with it."

What do you call a freezing bear?
A brrrrr.

What steps do you take if a tiger is coming toward you?
Big ones.

How many skunks does it take to make a big stink?
A phew.

Did you hear about the party at the Chinese zoo?
It was panda-monium.

Knock, knock.
Who's there?
Possum.
Possum who?
Possum food over here, please.

What did one bat say to the other?
"Let's hang out together."

Why don't anteaters get sick?
Because they're full of anty-bodies.

Why did the otter cross the road?
To get to the otter side.

Why don't bears wear shoes?
What's the use? They'd still have bear feet.

Why did the elephants get kicked out of the public pool?
They kept dropping their trunks.

Did you hear the joke about the skunk?
You don't want to—it really stinks.

What kind of music do sophisticated kangaroos listen to?
Hop-era.

What do you get when you cross a sheep and a porcupine?
An animal that can knit its own sweaters.

Knock, knock.
Who's there?
Gopher.
Gopher who?
Gopher a walk with me?

Why do gorillas have such big nostrils?
Because they have big fingers.

What do you call a flying skunk?
A smellicopter.

How do sick kangaroos get better?
They have a hop-eration.

Why are bears great at camping?
They only bring the bear necessities.

How did the panda lose his dinner?
He was bamboozled.

Knock, knock.
Who's there?
Kanga.
Kanga who?
No, it's kangaroo!

**What do you get when you cross
a kangaroo and a snake?**
A jump rope.

Why shouldn't you take a bear to the zoo?
Because they'd rather go to the movies.

Why did Sally bring her skunk to school?
For show-and-smell.

**What's the difference between
a flea and a coyote?**
One prowls on the hairy and the other howls
on the prairie.

**What do you call a
single buffalo?**
A buffalonely.

Knock, knock.
Who's there?
Gorilla.
Gorilla who?
Gorilla burger. I've got the buns!

**What do you get when you cross
a turtle and a porcupine?**
A slowpoke.

Why aren't koalas real bears?
They don't have the koalafications.

Why do tigers always eat raw meat?
They don't know how to cook.

What do you call a lazy baby kangaroo?
A pouch potato.

7

Slithery, Scaly Knee-Slappers

What's an alligator's favorite drink?
Gator-Ade.

What happened when the frog's car broke down on the side of the road?
It was toad away.

What do you get when you cross a snake with a tasty dessert?
A pie-thon!

What do you call an alligator who steals?
A crookodile.

What's a snake's favorite subject in school?
Hisssssstory.

**What do you get when you
cross a tortoise and a pig?**
A slowpork.

**Why did the snake laugh so
hard she started to cry?**
She thought the joke was hiss-terical.

Why are frogs such liars?
Because they are am-fib-ians.

What do you call a turtle that flies?
A shellicopter.

**What do you call a crocodile
that likes to go bowling?**
An alley-gator.

**What do you get when you cross
a canary and a 50-foot snake?**
A singalong.

Why did the frog say meow?
He was learning a foreign language.

How does a snake shoot something?
With a boa and arrows.

What do you call a famous turtle?
A shellebrity.

**If you crossed a snake and a robin,
what kind of bird would you get?**
A swallow.

Knock, knock.
Who's there?
Iguana.
Iguana who?
Iguana hold your hand.

What do you get when you cross a snake with a hot dog?
A fangfurter.

What's the difference between a dog and an alligator?
One's bark is worse than its bite.

Why are snakes always measured in inches?
Because they don't have feet.

**How does a frog feel when
he has a broken leg?**
Unhoppy.

**What do you get when you
cross a pig and a snake?**
A boar constrictor.

**What kind of snake keeps
its car the cleanest?**
A windshield viper.

**Which creature
has more lives
than a cat?**
A frog—they croak
every night.

What kind of photos do turtles take?
Shellfies.

What did the naughty little diamondback say to his sister?
"Don't be such a rattle-tail."

What do frogs do with paper?
Rip it, rip it.

Why don't alligators like fast food?
It's too hard to catch.

What's long, green, and goes "hith, hith"?
A snake with a lisp.

What do you get when you plant a frog?
A cr-oak tree.

**What did the frog say when he heard
"time flies when you are having fun?"**
"Time is fun when you're having flies!"

Customer: "Do you have alligator shoes?"
Clerk: "Yes, sir. What size does your alligator
wear?"

How do you weigh a snake?
With its scales.

What does a turtle do on its birthday?
It shellebrates.

**Which hand would you use to
pick up a dangerous snake?**
Someone else's.

What kind of shoes do frogs wear?
Open toad shoes.

What do you call a snake that builds things?
A boa constructor.

What did the snake give to his wife?
A goodnight hiss.

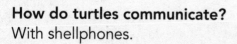

Why shouldn't you ever double-cross an alligator?
Because it may come back to bite you in the end.

How do turtles communicate?
With shellphones.

What do you call a snake with no clothes on?
S-naked.

What do you call an alligator in a vest?
An investigator.

In which river are you sure to find snakes?
The Hississippi River.

Knock, knock.
Who's there?
Thea.
Thea who?
Thea later, alligator.

What happens when two frogs collide?
They get tongue-tied.

Why are snakes so hard to fool?
You can't pull their legs.

What do you call an alligator with a GPS?
A navigator.

What's a snake's favorite dance?
The mamba.

Why are frogs always so happy?
They eat whatever bugs them.

8

Wacky Water Creatures

Where might orcas hear music?
Orca-stras!

Why do some fish live in salt water?
Because pepper makes them sneeze!

What kind of fish only swims at night?
A starfish.

Which day do fish hate?
Fryday!

Why would you bring a fish to a party?
Because it goes well with chips.

What did the sardine call the submarine?
A can of people.

What was King Arthur's favorite type of fish?
A swordfish.

How does a squid go into battle?
Well-armed.

What do you call a smelly fish?
A stink ray.

What do you get from a bad-tempered shark?
As far away as possible.

What's the difference between a piano and a fish?
You can tune a piano, but you can't tuna fish.

What does an octopus wear when it gets cold?
A coat of arms.

What birthday party game do fish like to play?
Salmon Says.

What do you call a messy crayfish?
A slobster.

Where do killer whales listen to music?
At the orca-stra.

What happened to the shark who swallowed a bunch of keys?
He got lockjaw.

Why are fish such intelligent creatures?
Because they swim in schools.

Why don't fish do well on school tests?
They work below C-level.

Who robs a bank and squirts ink?
Billy the Squid.

What do fish use for money?
Sand dollars.

What do whales like to chew?
Blubber gum.

Why did the fish blush?
It saw the ocean's bottom.

Did you know that an octopus is the only fish that can squirt ink?
Just squidding!

What do fish need to stay healthy?
Vitamin Sea.

Why do oysters go to the gym?
It's good for mussels.

What do you call a fish with no eye?
A fsh.

What's the saddest creature in the ocean?
A blue whale.

How many tickles does it take to make an octopus laugh?
Ten tickles.

Knock, knock.
Who's there?
Two knee.
Two knee who?
Two knee fish.

What's a dolphin's favorite kind of sandwich?
Peanut butter and jellyfish.

What do you get when you cross an elephant and a whale?
A submarine with a built-in snorkel.

What part of a fish weighs the most?
Its scales.

Where do dolphins sleep?
In waterbeds.

Where does a squid keep its money?
In its octopurse.

How do you make a goldfish old?
You take away the G.

How many shrimp did the seal eat?
A krillion.

**What do you call two octopuses
that look exactly alike?**
Itentacle.

Which fish swims in heaven?
An angelfish.

What's the best way to catch a fish?
Have someone throw one to you.

**What did Cinderella
Dolphin wear to the ball?**
Glass flippers.

How does a shellfish get to the hospital?
In a clambulance.

Which fish can perform medical operations?
A sturgeon.

Who held the octopus ransom?
Squidnappers.

9

Bonus Section:
Fossil Fun

What do you call a dinosaur with no eyes?
Doyouthinkysaraus.

How do you know if there is a dinosaur in your refrigerator?
The door won't shut!

What do dinosaurs use on the floors of their kitchens?
Rep-tiles.

Why was the Stegosaurus such a good volleyball player?
Because he could really spike the ball!

What's the nickname for someone who put their right hand in the mouth of a T-Rex?
Lefty.

What do you get when a dinosaur scores a touchdown?
A dino-score.

Why did the dinosaur cross the road?
To eat the chickens on the other side.

What do you call a sleeping dinosaur?
A dinosnore.

How do you raise a baby dinosaur?
With a crane.

What do you get when dinosaurs crash their cars?
Tyrannosaurus wrecks.

Which dinosaurs were the best police officers?
Triceracops.

What do you call a bruise on a T-Rex?
A dino-sore!

What makes more noise than a dinosaur?
Two dinosaurs.

Who makes dinosaur clothes?
A dino-sew-er.

What did dinosaurs have that no other animals had?
Baby dinosaurs.

What do you call a dinosaur that never gives up?
A try and try and try-ceratops!

What do dinosaurs use to cut wood?
A dinosaw.

What do you call a dinosaur that's a noisy sleeper?
A Bronto-snore-us.

**Where was the dinosaur when
the sun went down?**
In the dark.

What does a Triceratops sit on?
Its tricera-bottom.

What was the fastest dinosaur?
A pronto-saurus.

**What's the best way to talk
to a Tyrannosaur?**
Long distance.

**What do
dinosaurs eat on
camping trips?**
Dino-s'mores.

Why can't you hear
a Pterodactyl use
the bathroom?
Because the P is
silent.

**What should you do if you find
a dinosaur in your bed?**
Find somewhere else to sleep.

Why did the dinosaur cross the road?
The chicken wasn't around yet.

What does a Tyrannosaurus Rex eat?
Anything she wants!

**What do you call a dinosaur
who lost his glasses?**
Do-you-think-he-saur-us?

What do you call a dinosaur that eats fireworks?
A dinomite.

Why are there old dinosaur bones in the museum?
Because they can't afford new ones.

What has a spiked tail, plates on its back, and sixteen wheels?
A stegosaurus on roller skates.

When can three giant dinosaurs get under an umbrella and not get wet?
When it's not raining.

**What do you get when you cross
a triceratops and a kangaroo?**
A tricera-hops.

What came after the dinosaur?
Its tail.

**How to do make a
dinosaur float?**
Put a scoop of ice cream in
a glass of root beer and add
one dinosaur.

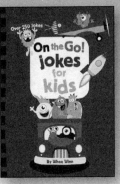